SO YOU THINK YOU KNOW TENNIS!

BY BURT CUTLER

Illustrations by Jack Bonestell

pss!

PRICE/STERN/SLOAN

Publishers, Inc.

1977

Library of Congress Catalog Card Number: 77-9457
ISBN: 0-8431-0427-9

THIS BOOK IS DEDICATED

*To Dr. Bill Horowitz, Ray Kovitz,
Jerry Schwartz and Irv Sitron who
have gallantly suffered my gamesmanship
and terrible calls these many years.*

*To George Taevs, who helped establish
the format for this book.*

*To Corey who may someday come to love
tennis as I do.*

*To the millions of fellow "hackers"
who derive great pleasure
from this splendid game.*

"He's not a very graceful loser."

PREFACE

There are over 30 million tennis players in the United States. Throughout the world, tennis is becoming the number one sport; surely it already has become the number one *outdoor* sport!

One of the unique things about tennis is that (with no umpire present) the player is expected to call his opponent's shots "in" or "out" *on his own side*! Thus tennis is still considered a gentleman's (or gentlewoman's) game because a player is required to give the benefit of any doubt to his/her opponent.

Add the fact that most tennis players don't know the basic rules of tennis, and you have a basis for *mayhem.*

This book will NOT free the reader from frustrations due to playing ability, BUT it should free him from protracted arguments over tennis rules.

HOW TENNIS DEVELOPED

Tennis, in different forms, has been around for a long time. Some sports historians trace it all the way back to the ancient Greeks. No one really knows. We do know for sure that *similar* games were played in medieval France and England; in fact, a likely derivation of the name "tennis" is from the French *Tenez!* ("Get ready!" or "Pay attention!").

Modern tennis actually began approximately 100 years ago when a Major Wingfield of England invented a new type of tennis game to jazz up his lawn party. His new game (using an hourglass-shaped court and a net almost as tall as a badminton net) — which until then had been played exclusively by royalty — brought tennis down to the merely well-to-do. Tennis remained a sport for the elite for many years; even in America in the 1920's and 1930's tennis was played almost exclusively at the clubs of the rich. And now look at it — even you and I can play!

WHO NEEDS THIS BOOK?

Anyone who plays tennis *without an umpire or linesmen* needs this book. That includes 99.8% of all tennis players.

SO YOU THINK YOU KNOW TENNIS is a great gift for any tennis-playing friend, including yourself. The longer a person has played tennis the greater the shock at learning that he or she *doesn't know the rules!*

May we also suggest that, after reading this book, you keep it in your tote bag for handy reference on the court.

SCORE YOURSELF

This book contains a series of questions and answers on some of the fine points of tennis. The official rules are condensed in the back of the book for further reference.

As you read each QUESTION, cover the ANSWER and don't look at it until you've chosen your own.

Score yourself.

A first-time score of 25 or more is excellent. However, if you're part of the 99 out of 100 people who score poorly the first time, don't panic. Reread and check yourself until you know *all* the answers.

QUESTION 1

Is it ever legal to hit the ball on your opponent's side of the net?

ANSWER

Yes! Most people think you can *never* reach over the net. However, there *are* situations where it's legal.

It is, of course, illegal to reach over the net and hit the ball *before* it bounces on your side.

Consider this, though. If player A hits the ball with enough spin so that it lands in B's court and bounces back into A's court, player B may — after the ball bounces on her side — reach over the net and hit it! (This rule applies whether the ball comes back due to spin or heavy wind.)

QUESTION 2

A player lunges after a ball; the racket slips out of his hand and hits the ball back into the opponent's court! Since the player was not touching the racket at the point of contact, is it a fair play?

ANSWER

No. To be a good point, the racket must be *held* while the ball is hit.

QUESTION 3

Are there any situations where it is o.k. for your body or clothing to touch the net while ball is in play?

ANSWER

No. The rules state that no part of your body, clothing (or racket) can touch the net *at any time* while ball is in play. If it does, you're penalized by losing the point.

QUESTION 4

It often happens that a ball is returned from outside the court. In that event, it must either pass over the net, or over an imaginary extension of the net to be considered a good return.

True or False?

ANSWER

False. If a ball is hit from beyond the side-line, it is possible to return it *outside* of the net; in that event, it does *not* have to pass over the imaginary extension of the top of the net.

For example, it can reach a maximum height of only a foot above the court, as long as it touches down fairly in the opponent's court.

QUESTION 5

The ball hits the post holding the net, then goes over the net and lands "in." Is it a good return?

ANSWER

Yes. The ball can hit the post, but it must then pass *over* the net to be a good return. The rally continues because the net post is considered part of the net.

(This isn't too unfair when you consider that usually this will occur when the ball is hit from *outside* the sideline and is en route to an otherwise clean return.)

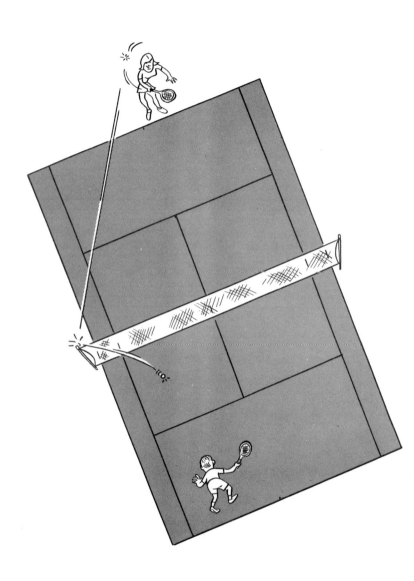

QUESTION 6

On a *serve*, the ball hits the post and then lands within the proper service court.

Is it considered

a)   a let ball?

b)   a service fault?

c)   a good service?

ANSWER

b)   it's a service fault

Different rules apply to a ball hitting the net post during play than while serving.

It is a service fault if the ball touches any permanent fixture (except the net, strap or band) before it hits the ground.

(Considering the angle from which a serve is required to be delivered, it would be unfair to have a clearly wayward service receive the benefit of an obviously freakish bounce.)

A

B

24

QUESTION 7

Player A hits the ball on her side of the net. After the ball leaves her racket, the follow-through of her swing carries the racket over the net into player B's court.

Is it a legitimate stroke?

ANSWER

Yes. This is a fair play. The racket *can* pass over the net, but on a volley it must not make contact with the ball on the opponent's side.

QUESTION 8

In matches played without umpire or linesmen, who should determine whether the service was in or out?

a) the receiver
b) the server

(How about in doubles?)

ANSWER

a)   The receiver determines whether the service is good or a fault.

(In doubles, the receiver's partner should make the calls with respect to the service line.)

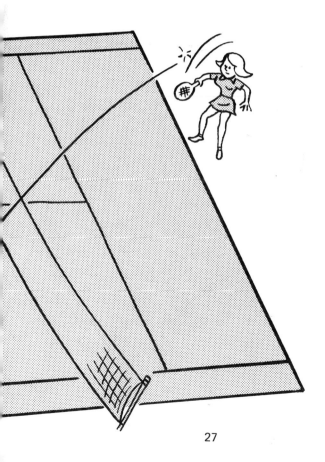

QUESTION 9

It's illegal to deliver an underhand serve.

True or False?

ANSWER

False. It is perfectly legal to use an underhand serve.

Some hackers have developed very tricky underhand spin serves for their bags of tricks.

(Also useful for players with bad backs who can't arch their backs for a hard overhead serve.)

QUESTION 10

It's legal to bounce-hit the ball on a serve (bounce the ball and immediately hit it).

True or False?

ANSWER

False. It's illegal.

For a serve to be legal, the ball must not touch the ground before it's hit.

QUESTION 11

Player A serves the ball to player B. The ball hits B. It is A's point because B allowed himself to be hit.

True or False?

ANSWER

True. The receiver has the responsibility of not being hit on the serve . . . no matter *where* he's standing!!

QUESTION 12

Which of the following are official regulations for tennis balls?

a) must be 2 1/2" — 2 5/8" in diameter.

b) must weigh between 2 and 2 1/16 ozs.

c) must bounce 53 to 58 inches when dropped 100" on a concrete base.

d) must have a forward deformation of .220 to .290 inches when subjected to a pressure of 18 lbs.

e) must have a thickness of fuzz of 1/16" to 3/32".

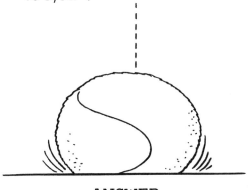

ANSWER

a, b, c, and d are among the regulations; e is not.

QUESTION 13

The server can step on the baseline, but his toes cannot project beyond it.

True or False?

ANSWER

False. It is considered a service fault if either foot touches *any* part of the baseline before the ball is hit.

QUESTION 14

On service, a player *misses* the ball entirely; this is a fault, the same penalty as if the ball had been hit into the net.

True or False?

ANSWER

True. A complete miss while attempting to serve is a fault.

QUESTION 15

The server is allowed to walk or run while making service delivery, as long as the base line is not passed.

True or False?

ANSWER

False. The server *cannot* change position by walking or running; if she does, it's a foot fault.

(Recently revised rules permit a player to swing a foot over the baseline in air; the server is also permitted to jump off the ground while serving.)

QUESTION 16

Player A serves to player B. His serve hits the net, then hits B. B is standing between the service and base lines.

Is it

    a)   a point for the server?

    b)   a service let (to be replayed)?

    c)   a point for the receiver?

    d)   a fault?

ANSWER

b)   It's a let; the serve is replayed.

B

QUESTION 17

Player B is receiving a serve. He isn't ready, but tries to return the ball at the last moment and misses. He then complains that he wasn't ready. According to the rules, he was "ready" because he tried to return the ball.

True or False?

ANSWER

True. If you're not ready, you should let the ball go by.

QUESTION 18

A player hits the ball immediately after it has bounced out of bounds so he claims the point.

Is it his point or does the ball remain in play because he hit it?

ANSWER

Common practice permits a player to call a shot on his side (unless there's a linesman or or umpire present). Thus, if he calls the ball out, it's considered out — and it's his point. It doesn't matter that he hit the ball — play was dead as soon as the ball landed out. BUT he must make that "out" call *immediately* — not after waiting to see how the point came out!

QUESTION 19

A player volleys the ball while standing just *beyond* the baseline. Realizing that the ball was out of bounds, she yells "out" just as she volleys it.

Is it her point?

ANSWER

No. It is *not* her point. The play must continue as if the ball had landed inside the baseline.

This is a different situation than the previous question. In the other case, the player actually *sees* the ball land out of bounds and play is dead as of that moment.

A player must let the ball land to prove that it was actually out.

QUESTION 20

A player hits the ball so that it comes off the racket with the effect of a "sling" or a "throw." The other player claims her opponent "carried" the ball and therefore should lose the point.

Is a "carry" a good hit?

ANSWER

A player may not "touch or strike the ball in play with his racket more than once in making a stroke."

This is fairly easy to interpret if the ball comes off the racket and then takes an obvious second trajectory. It is also illegal (but more difficult to judge) if the effect is a sling or throw. Such strokes are called "double hits" or "carries."

This is a most difficult call even for an umpire. The general guideline for umpires is that if the player who stroked the ball doesn't volunteer that it was a carry, the umpire will give the player the benefit of the doubt— unless the umpire clearly sees the player give a "second-push" to the ball.

Without an umpire present, in the case of a dispute, it's good practice to let the player who hit the ball judge whether in fact it was a carry or a double hit.

QUESTION 21

In doubles play, if a server's ball hits either of the opposing players before hitting the ground, it is

a) a good point for the server
b) a service fault
c) a let ball
d) a point for the opposing team

ANSWER

a)   A point for the server . . . This rule
applies for singles as well as doubles.

QUESTION 22

The rules state that if a partner serves out of turn, the partner who should have served will do so as soon as the mistake is discovered.

Do the points played before the mistake was discovered stand as played?

ANSWER

Yes, all points scored (and any faults served) up to the time the mistake was discovered shall be "reckoned" (counted).

QUESTION 23

An entire game is completed with the wrong player serving. At the end of the game, the players realize the error.

Does the game count?

ANSWER

Yes, the game counts; but the order of service will thereafter *remain as changed.*

QUESTION 24

In singles play, service from the wrong half of the court occurs; when this is discovered

a)   the points count as played.

b)   the game is forfeited.

c)   the server should continue serving wherever he happens to be serving at the time the error is discovered.

d)   the server should continue serving, moving to the correct side for the score as now understood.

ANSWER

a) and d) are correct.

QUESTION 25

A volley which is clearly going out of bounds hits a player. Whose point is it?

ANSWER

The player who gets hit loses the point.

STAY OUT OF THE WAY!

QUESTION 26

Player A yells at her opponent just before player B hits the ball. Player B misses the ball and protests that player A distracted her and thus interfered.

Is it

a) a point for A?

b) a point for B?

c) point is replayed?

d) who knows?

A   B

ANSWER

c) The first time player B does this the point could be replayed if it was truly an involuntary outcry. But any deliberate outcry — or B's "second offense" — should result in awarding the point to A.

"Interference" is often a difficult judgement call. For example, in doubles, the server's partner who is playing net may feint moving toward center court; once the ball is in play, this, or any other feinting action (taken with the whole body) is o.k. However, examples of "questionable tactics" would be

1) The server's partner at the net throws up his non-racket arm as a feint just as the receiver is returning the serve.

2) The receiver's partner (who is standing half way to the net) starts to run up to the net while the server is tossing up the ball.

Both of the above are clearly unnecessarily distracting, and although not specifically prohibited by the rules — are poor sportsmanship and should be self-regulated by the players' common agreement.

QUESTION 27

A ball being played or served hits another ball lying in the court. Because of this the receiver cannot return the ball.

Is it a point, or does the play go over?

ANSWER

Seems unfair, but the point stands — if it was a ball that had been lying there at the time the point was started. Better get loose balls out of the way! (Note: It also may save a broken arm, leg or ankle!)

QUESTION 28

You swing at the ball; instead of hitting it with your racket face, you hit it with the fingers that are holding the racket. Otherwise, it's a clean return.

Is this return legal or illegal?

ANSWER

It's illegal. The point is over as soon as the ball hits *any part* of a player's body or clothing.

However, it *is* a good return if the ball is returned against (only) the racket handle.

QUESTION 29

If your return hits a light standard on the fly and then bounces "in," it

a)   is a point for the opponent
b)   should be replayed
c)   is your point if not returned

ANSWER

a)   If the ball hits a light standard (or any other non-net permanent fixture), it's a lost point for the player who hit it.

QUESTION 30

In a tournament game, a player arrives with a large ping-pong paddle and starts to play. Can he get away with this?

ANSWER

Yes! Unlike strict regulations on tennis balls, there is *no* restriction on the size or composition of a tennis racket (as of August, 1977).

QUESTION 31

A "let" is

a) a served ball that touches the net, yet lands in the proper service area

b) any situation which requires the point to be replayed

c) either of the above

ANSWER

c) is correct. Note that a service let on *second* service does not mean the entire point is to be replayed; the server gets to try again with his second service.

QUESTION 32

Which of these are correct?
The service is a let if

a) the ball touches the net and then hits the receiver before hitting the ground

b) the ball touches the net but is a good service otherwise

c) a service or service fault is delivered when the receiver is not ready.

ANSWER

a), b), and c) are all correct.

QUESTION 33

Is it allowable in doubles for the server's partner to stand in a position that obstructs the view of the receiver?

ANSWER

Yes. The server's partner may take any position on his side of the net (in or out of the court) that he wishes. (The same is true of the receiver's partner).

RULES OF TENNIS

AND

SELECTED CASES AND DECISIONS*

EXPLANATORY NOTE

The appended Code of Rules, and Cases and Decisions is the Official Code of the International Lawn Tennis Federation, of which the United States Tennis Association is a member.

DIAGRAM AND DIMENSIONS OF TENNIS COURT

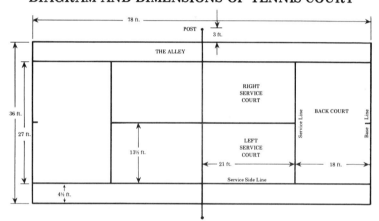

THE SINGLES GAME

RULE 1: DIMENSIONS AND EQUIPMENT

The court shall be a rectangle 78 feet (23.77m) long and 27 feet (8.23m) wide. It shall be divided across the middle by a net suspended from a cord or metal cable of a maximum diameter of one-third of an inch (0.8cm), the ends of which shall be attached to, or pass over, the tops of two posts, 3 feet 6 inches (1.07m) high, and not more than 6 inches (15cm) in diameter, the centers of which shall be 3 feet (0.91m) outside the court on each side. The net shall be extended fully so that it fills completely the space between the two posts and shall be of sufficiently small mesh to prevent the ball's passing through. The height of the net shall be 3 feet (0.914m) at the center, where it shall be held down taut by a strap not more than 2 inches (5cm) wide and

*Reprinted with permission of the United States Tennis Association, Incorporated. Portions of the Rules, Cases and Decisions and USTA Examples and Comments have been deleted for brevity. The complete set of Rules and Interpretations can be obtained from USTA, 71 University Place, Princeton, N. J. 08540.

white in color. There shall be a band covering the cord or metal cable and the top of the net for not less than 2 inches (5cm) nor more than 2½ inches (6.3cm) in depth on each side and white in color. There shall be no advertisement on the net, strap, band or singles sticks. The lines bounding the ends and sides of the Court shall respectively be called the Baselines and the Sidelines. On each side of the net, at a distance of 21 feet (6.40m) from it and parallel with it, shall be drawn the Service lines. The space on each side of the net between the service line and the sidelines shall be divided into two equal parts, called the service courts, by the center service line, which must be 2 inches (5cm) in width, drawn half-way between, and parallel with, the sidelines. Each baseline shall be bisected by an imaginary continuation of the center service line to a line 4 inches (10cm) in length and 2 inches (5cm) in width called the center mark, drawn inside the Court at right angles to and in contact with such baselines. All other lines shall be not less than 1 inch (2.5cm) nor more than 2 inches (5cm) in width, except the baseline, which may be 4 inches (10cm) in width, and all measurements shall be made to the outside of the lines.

RULE 2 : PERMANENT FIXTURES

The permanent fixtures of the Court shall include not only the net, posts, cord or metal cable, strap and band, but also, where there are any such, the back and side stops, the stands, fixed or movable seats and chairs around the Court, and their occupants, all other fixtures around and above the Court, and the Umpire, Net-cord Judge, Foot-fault Judge, Linesman and Ball Boys when in their respective places.

RULE 3 : BALL — SIZE, WEIGHT AND BOUND

The ball shall have a uniform outer surface and shall be white or yellow in color. If there are any seams they shall be stitchless. The ball shall be more than two and a half inches (6.35cm) and less than two and five-eighths inches (6.67cm) in diameter, and more than two ounces (56.7 grams) and less than two and one-sixteenth ounces (58.5 grams) in weight. The ball shall have a bound of more than 53 inches (135cm) and less than 58 inches (147cm) when dropped 100 inches (254cm) upon a concrete base. The ball shall have a forward deformation of more than .220 of an inch (.56cm) and less than .290 of an inch (.74cm) and a return deformation of more than .350 of an inch (.89cm) and less than .425 of an inch (1.08cm) at 18 lbs. (8.165 kg) load. The two deformation figures shall be the averages of three individual readings along three axes of the ball and no two individual readings shall differ by more than .030 of an inch (.08cm) in each case. All tests for bound, size and deformation shall be made in accordance with the regulations in the Appendix hereto.

RULE 4 : SERVER AND RECEIVER

The Players shall stand on opposite sides of the net; the player who first delivers the ball shall be called the Server, and the other the Receiver.

RULE 5: CHOICE OF ENDS AND SERVICE

The choice of ends and the right to be Server or Receiver in the first game shall be decided by toss. The player winning the toss may choose, or require his opponent to choose:

(a) The right to be Server or Receiver, in which case the other player shall choose the end; or

(b) The end, in which case the other player shall choose the right to be Server or Receiver.

RULE 6: DELIVERY OF SERVICE

The service shall be delivered in the following manner. Immediately before commencing to serve, the Server shall stand with both feet at rest behind (i.e. farther from the net than) the base-line, and within the imaginary continuations of the center-mark and side-line. The Server shall then project the ball by hand into the air in any direction and before it hits the ground strike it with his racket, and the delivery shall be deemed to have been completed at the moment of the impact of the racket and the ball. A player with the use of only one arm may utilize his racket for the projection.

Case 1. May the Server in a singles game take his stand behind the portion of the base-line between the sidelines of the singles court and the doubles court?
Decision. No.
Case 3. May a player serve underhand?
Decision. Yes. There is no restriction regarding the kind of service which may be used; that is, the player may use an underhand or overhand service at his discretion.

RULE 7: FOOT FAULT

The Server shall throughout the delivery of the service:

(a) Not change his position by walking or running.

(b) Not touch, with either foot, any area other than that behind the base-line within the imaginary extension of the center-mark and side-line.

Note: The Server shall not, by slight movements of the feet which do not materially affect the location originally taken up by him, be deemed "to change his position by walking or running."

RULE 8: FROM ALTERNATE COURTS

(a) In delivering the service, the Server shall stand alternately behind the right and left Courts, beginning from the right in every game. If service from a wrong half of the Court occurs and is undetected, all play resulting from such wrong service or services shall stand, but the inaccuracy of the station shall be corrected immediately it is discovered.

(b) The ball served shall pass over the net and hit the ground within the Service Court which is diagonally opposite, or upon any line bounding such Court, before the Receiver returns it.

COMMENT: The Receiver is not allowed to volley a served ball, i.e., he must allow it to strike in his court first. (See Rule 16(a).)

EXPLANATION: In matches played without umpire or linesmen, it is customary for the Receiver to determine whether the service is good or a fault; indeed, each player makes the calls for all balls hit to his side of the net. (In doubles, the Receiver's partner makes the calls with respect to the service line.)

RULE 9: FAULTS

The Service is a fault:

(a) If the Server commit any breach of Rules 6, 7 or 8;

(b) If he miss the ball in attempting to strike it;

(c) If the ball served touch a permanent fixture (other than the net, strap or band) before it hits the ground.

Case 1. After throwing a ball up preparatory to serving, the Server decides not to strike at it and catches it instead. Is it a fault?

Decision. No.

RULE 10: SERVICE AFTER A FAULT

After a fault (if it be the first fault) the Server shall serve again from behind the same half of the Court from which he served that fault, unless the service was from the wrong half, when. in accordance with Rule 8, the Server shall be entitled to one service only from behind the other half. A fault may not be claimed after the next service has been delivered.

RULE 11: RECEIVER MUST BE READY

The Server shall not serve until the Receiver is ready. If the latter attempt to return the service, he shall be deemed ready. If, however, the Receiver signify that he is not ready, he may not claim a fault because the ball does not hit the ground within the limits fixed for the service.

RULE 12: A LET

NOTE: A service that touches the net in passing yet falls into the proper court is a let. This word is used also when, because of an interruption while the ball is in play, or for any other reason, a point is to be replayed.

In all cases where a let has to be called under the rules, or to provide for an interruption to play, it shall have the following interpretations:

(a) When called solely in respect of a service, that one service only shall be replayed.

(b) When called under any other circumstance, the point shall be replayed.

RULE 13: THE SERVICE IS A LET

The service is a let:

(a) If the ball served touch the net, strap or band, and is otherwise good, or, after touching the net, strap or band, touch the Receiver or anything which he wears or carries before hitting the ground.

(b) If a service or a fault be delivered when the Receiver is not ready (see Rule 11).

73

RULE 14 : WHEN RECEIVER BECOMES SERVER

At the end of the first game the Receiver shall become the Server, and the Server Receiver; and so on alternately in all the subsequent games of a match. If a player serve out of turn, the player who ought to have served shall serve as soon as the mistake is discovered, but all points scored before such discovery shall be reckoned. If a game shall have been completed before such discovery, the order of service remains as altered. A fault served before such discovery shall not be reckoned.

RULE 15 : BALL IN PLAY TILL POINT DECIDED

A ball is in play from the moment at which it is delivered in service. Unless a fault or a let be called, it remains in play until the point is decided.

RULE 16 : SERVER WINS POINT

The Server wins the point:

(a) If the ball served, not being a let under Rule 13, touch the Receiver or anything which he wears or carries, before it hits the ground;

(b) If the Receiver otherwise loses the point as provided by Rule 18.

RULE 17 : RECEIVER WINS POINT

The Receiver wins the point:

(a) If the Server serve two consecutive faults;

(b) If the Server otherwise lose the point as provided by Rule 18

RULE 18 : PLAYER LOSES POINT

A player loses the point if:

(a) He fail, before the ball in play has hit the ground twice consecutively, to return it directly over the net (except as provided in Rule 22(a) or (c)); or

(b) He return the ball in play so that it hits ground, a permanent fixture. or other object, outside any of the lines which bound his opponent's Court (except as provided in Rule 22 (a) and (c)); or

(c) He volley the ball and fail to make a good return even when standing outside the Court; or

(d) He touch or strike the ball in play with his racket more than once in making a stroke; or

EXPLANATION: A player may be deemed to have touched the ball more than once if the ball takes an obvious second trajectory as it comes off the racket, or comes off the racket in such a way that the effect is that of a "sling" or "throw" rather than that of a "hit." Such strokes are informally referred to as "double hits" or "carries." Experienced umpires give the player the benefit of the doubt unless they see such a second trajectory or a definite "second push."

(e) He or his racket (in his hand or otherwise) or anything which he wears or carries touch the net, posts, cord or metal cable, strap or band, or the ground within his opponent's Court at any time while the ball is in play; or

(f) He volley the ball before it has passed the net; or

(g) The ball in play touch him or anything that he wears or carries, except his racket in his hand or hands; or

(h) He throws his racket at and hits the ball.

Note: Case 7 of 7 cases is particularly of interest: A player standing outside the court volleys the ball or catches it in his hand and claims the point because the ball was certainly going out of court.

Decision. In no circumstance can he claim the point;

(1) If he catches the ball he loses the point under Rule 18 (g).

(2) If he volleys it and makes a bad return he loses the point under Rule 18 (c).

(3) If he volleys it and makes a good return, the rally continues.

RULE 19 : PLAYER HINDERS OPPONENT

If a player commits any act either deliberate or involuntary which, in the opinion of the Umpire, hinders his opponent in making a stroke, the Umpire shall in the first case award the point to the opponent, and in the second case order the point to be replayed.

RULE 20 : BALL FALLING ON LINE — GOOD

A ball falling on a line is regarded as falling in the Court bounded by that line.

COMMENT: In matches played without officials, it is customary for each player to make the calls on all balls hit to his side of the net.

RULE 21 : BALL TOUCHING PERMANENT FIXTURE

If the ball in play touch a permanent fixture (other than the net, posts, cord or metal cable, strap or band) after it has hit the ground, the player who struck it wins the point; if before it hits the ground his opponent wins the point.

RULE 22 : GOOD RETURN

It is a good return:

(a) If the ball touch the net, posts, cord or metal cable, strap or band, provided that it passes over any of them and hits the ground within the Court; or

(b) If the ball, served or returned, hit the ground within the proper Court and rebound or be blown back over the net, and the player whose turn it is to strike reach over the net and play the ball, provided that neither he nor any part of his clothes or racket touch the net, posts, cord or metal cable, strap or band or the ground within his opponent's Court, and that the stroke be otherwise good; or

(c) If the ball be returned outside the post, either above or below the level of the top of the net, even though it touch the post, provided that it hits the ground within the proper Court; or

(d) If a player's racket pass over the net after he has returned the ball, provided the ball pass the net before being played and be properly returned; or

(e) If a player succeeded in returning the ball, served or in play, which strikes a ball lying in the Court.

Note.—If, for the sake of convenience, a doubles court be equipped with singles posts for the purpose of singles game, then the doubles posts and those portions of the net, cord or metal cable and band outside such singles posts shall be regarded as "permanent fixtures *other than* net, post, strap or band," and therefore *not* posts or parts of the net of that singles game.

A return that passes under the net cord between the singles and adjacent doubles post without touching either net cord, net or doubles post and falls within the area of play, is a good return. (But in doubles this would be a through" — loss of point.)

RULE 23 : INTERFERENCE

In case a player is hindered in making a stroke by anything not within his control except a permanent fixture of the Court, or except as provided for in Rule 19, the point shall be replayed.

RULE 24 : THE GAME

If a player wins his first point, the score is called *15* for that player; on winning his second point, the score is called *30* for that player; on winning his third point, the score is called *40* for that player, and the fourth point won by a player is scored *game* for that player except as below:

If both players have won three points, the score is called *deuce;* and the next point won by a player is called *advantage for that player.* If the same player wins the next point, he wins the game; if the other player wins the next point the score is again called *deuce;* and so on until a player wins the two points immediately following the score at deuce, when the game is scored for that player.

RULE 25 : THE SET

A player (or players) who first wins six games wins a set; except that he must win by a margin of two games over his opponent and where necessary a set shall be extended until this margin be achieved. NOTE: See tiebreaker.

RULE 26 : WHEN PLAYERS CHANGE ENDS

The players shall change ends at the end of the first, third and every subsequent alternative game of each set, and at the end of each set unless the total number of games in such set be even, in which case the change is not made until the end of the first game of the next set.

RULE 27 : MAXIMUM NUMBER OF SETS

The maximum number of sets in a match shall be 5, or, where women take part, 3.

RULE 28: RULES APPLY TO BOTH SEXES

Except where otherwise stated, every reference in these Rules to the masculine includes the feminine gender.

RULE 29: DECISIONS OF UMPIRE AND REFEREE

In matches where a Chair Umpire is appointed his decision shall be final; but where a Referee is appointed an appeal shall lie to him from the decision of a Chair Umpire on a question of law, and in all such cases the decision of the Referee shall be final.

In matches where assistants to the Chair Umpire are appointed (Line Umpires, Net Umpire, Foot-fault Judge) their decisions shall be final on questions of fact. When such an assistant is unable to give a decision he shall indicate this immediately to the Chair Umpire who shall give a decision. When the Chair is unable to give a decision on a question of fact he shall order a let to be called.

In Davis Cup and Wightman Cup and Bonne Bell Cup matches only, the decision of an assistant to the Chair Umpire, or the Chair Umpire if the assistant is unable to make a decision, can be changed by the Referee, who may also authorize the Chair Umpire to change the decision of an assistant or order a let to be called.

The Referee, in his discretion, may at any time postpone a match on account of darkness or the condition of the ground or the weather. In any case of postponement the previous score and previous occupancy of courts shall hold good, unless the Referee and the players unanimously agree otherwise.

RULE 30

Play shall be continuous from the first service till the match be concluded; provided that after the third set or when women take part, the second set, either player is entitled to a rest, which shall not exceed 10 minutes, or in countries situated between Latitude 15 degrees North and Latitude 15 degrees South, 45 minutes, and provided further that when necessitated by circumstances not within the control of the players, the Umpire may suspend play for such a period as he may consider necessary. If play be suspended and be not resumed until a later day the rest may be taken only after the third set (or when women take part the second set) of play on such later day, completion of an unfinished set being counted as one set. These provisions shall be strictly construed, and play shall never be suspended, delayed or interfered with for the purpose of enabling a player to recover his strength or his wind, or to receive instruction or advice. The Chair Umpire shall be the sole judge of such suspension, delay or interference, and after giving due warning he may disqualify the offender.

THE DOUBLES GAME
RULE 31

The above Rules shall apply to the Doubles Game except as below.

RULE 32: DIMENSIONS OF COURT

For the Doubles Game the Court shall be 36 feet (10.97m) in width, i.e. 4½ feet (1.37m) wider on each side than the Court for the Singles Game, and those portions of the singles sidelines which lie between the two service lines shall be called the service sidelines. In other respects, the Court shall be similar to that described in Rule 1, but the portions of the singles sidelines between the baseline and the service line on each side of the net may be omitted if desired.

Case 1. In doubles the Server claims the right to stand at the corner of the court as marked by the doubles side line. Is the foregoing correct or is it necessary that the Server stand within the limits of the center mark and the singles side line?

Decision. The Server has the right to stand anywhere between the center mark and the doubles sideline.

RULE 33: ORDER OF SERVICE

The order of serving shall be decided at the beginning of each set as follows:

The pair who have to serve in the first game of each set shall decide which partner shall do so and the opposing pair shall decide similarly for the second game. The partner of the player who served in the first game shall serve in the third; the partner of the player who served in the second game shall serve in the fourth, and so on in the same order in all the subsequent games of a set.

EXPLANATION: It is not required that the order of service, as between partners, carry over from one set to the next. Each team is allowed to decide which partner shall serve first for it, in each set. This same option applies with respect to the order of receiving service.

RULE 34: ORDER OF RECEIVING

The order of receiving the service shall be decided at the beginning of each set as follows:

The pair who have to receive the service in the first game shall decide which partner shall receive the first service, and that partner shall continue to receive the first service in every odd game throughout that set. The opposing pair shall likewise decide which partner shall receive the first service in the second game and that partner shall continue to receive the first service in every even game throughout that set. Partners shall receive the service alternately throughout each game.

EXPLANATION: The receiving formation of a doubles team may not be changed during a set; only at the start of a new set. Partners must receive throughout each set on the same sides of the court which they originally select when the set began. The first Server is not required to receive in the right court; he may select either side, but must hold this to the end of the set.

Case 1. Is it allowable in doubles for the Server's partner to stand in a position that obstructs the view of the Receiver?

Decision. Yes. The Server's partner may take any position on his side of the net in or out of the court that he wishes. (The same is true of the Receiver's partner.)

RULE 35: SERVICE OUT OF TURN

If a partner serve out of his turn, the partner who ought to have served shall serve as soon as the mistake is discovered, but all points scored, and any faults served before such discovery shall be reckoned. If a game shall have been completed before such discovery the order of service remains as altered.

RULE 36: ERROR IN ORDER OF RECEIVING

If during a game the order of receiving the service is changed by the receivers it shall remain as altered until the end of the game in which the mistake is discovered, but the partners shall resume their original order of receiving in the next game of that set in which they are receivers of the service.

RULE 37: BALL TOUCHING SERVER'S PARTNER IS FAULT

The service is a fault as provided for by Rule 9, or if the ball served touch the Server's partner or anything he wears or carries; but if the ball served touch the partner of the Receiver or anything which he wears or carries, not being a let under Rule 13 (a), before it hits the ground, the Server wins the point.

RULE 38: BALL STRUCK ALTERNATELY

The ball shall be struck alternately by one or other player of the opposing pairs, and if a player touches the ball in play with his racket in conravention of this Rule, his opponents win the point.

pss!

PRICE/STERN/SLOAN
Publishers, Inc., Los Angeles